Deleg
Skills
for Teachers

Professional Skills for Teachers series

Team-building with Teachers, Judith Chivers
Presentation Skills for Teachers, Jean M Harris
Delegation Skills for Teachers, Jim Knight
Time Management for Teachers, Ian Nelson

This practical series is aimed specifically at developing teachers' management skills. The books include activities and suggestions for things to do, to encourage the reader to think about their own needs and experiences. It will be helpful to have pen and paper handy to write down notes or ideas as you read.

Delegation Skills for Teachers

JIM KNIGHT

KOGAN
PAGE

London • Philadelphia

First published in 1995

Apart from any fair dealing for the purposes of research or private study, or criticism or review, as permitted under the Copyright, Designs and Patents Act, 1988, this publication may only be reproduced, stored or transmitted, in any form or by any means, with the prior permission in writing of the publishers, or in the case of reprographic reproduction in accordance with the terms of licences issued by the Copyright Licensing Agency. Enquiries concerning reproduction outside those terms should be sent to the publishers at the undermentioned address:

Kogan Page Limited
120 Pentonville Road
London N1 9JN

© Jim Knight, 1995

British Library Cataloguing in Publication Data

A CIP record for this book is available from the British Library.

ISBN 0 7494 1727 7

Typeset by Saxon Graphics Ltd, Derby
Printed and bound in Great Britain by Biddles Ltd, Guildford and King's Lynn.

Contents

Contents

Preface

The meaning of delegation

Delegate is defined, in Chambers Twentieth Century Dictionary, as: 'To send as a legate or representative: to entrust or commit'. The Shorter Oxford offers more, and more detailed, definitions but they mean the same: 'To send or commission (a person) as a deputy or representative, with power to act for another; to entrust or commit (authority) etc. to another as agent or deputy'. Delegation, in the specific sense to which this book is directed, obviously owes something to these fundamental definitions, but no standard dictionary recognizes delegation as carrying a meaning specifically defined in terms of management. Within the management lexicon itself, however, delegation has acquired the status of a 'concept'. It is represented as an idea with a common meaning for those who utilize it. From this it is assumed that the actions which flow from its application will be largely similar; in practice this is frequently far from true.

As with many other words used by managers, 'delegation' is a word which is at least as frequently misunderstood or misapplied as it is used accurately or comprehended precisely in practice. It is also used in at least two different contexts – to describe a particular *style* of management and to denote a *tool or tactic* in management: each of these contexts has a bearing upon the meaning conveyed when the word is used. Hence the word delegation, at least as used in management, has no one precise, comprehensible meaning despite the frequency with which it is used: it lacks an operational definition.

'What is an operational definition? An operational definition puts communicable meaning into a concept'. So said W Edwards Deming, a great American exponent of the key responsibilities of managers. He went on to say, 'An operational definition is one that reasonable men can agree on'.

Regarding the two contexts referred to above, this book is concerned with *delegation as a tool or tactic of management,* although its purpose will not be met without at least some reference to the concepts which have led researchers to use the term to describe a particular style of management: more of that later. However, the word 'management' itself requires operational definition. Although it is now far more regularly used within schools and colleges, my experience suggests that it is still used with great reluctance, sometimes with cynicism, or often pejoratively.

The feeling remains prevalent in many schools that teaching, because it has many of the features of an art form, is somehow above and beyond an activity as mundane and functional as management. It is not the purpose of this book to join that debate. However, because of it, it is important that any reader of this book understands what my operational definition of management is:

> Management is achieving goals by, with and through people and managers are all those responsible for the work of other adults. (DES, 1990)

Thus, to me, management implies a group of people working together within an organization, one of whom has accepted an overall responsibility for the work of that group. Therefore, whenever delegation is used in this book, three key elements will be presumed present in the mind of the reader:

❏ a person who has accepted responsibility for supporting and supervising the work of others – the 'manager'. Most typically in schools/colleges this will be a head of department, curriculum coordinator, deputy head, headteacher, principal, etc.

❏ another person or a group of others through and with whom that work is conducted; typically in schools/colleges the colleagues in that particular department, section or school for which the teacher-manager is responsible

❏ an organization – a department, school or college – to the achievement of whose purposes all those concerned owe their professional allegiance.

In sum, delegation only has 'communicable meaning' here within the contexts of management (accepting responsibility for work done through and with a group of others) within organizational structures.

References

Out of the Crisis, W Edwards Deming, CUP, 1986.
Developing School Management: The way forward, School Management Task Force, DES, HMSO, 1990.

CHAPTER I

What Delegation Is – and Is Not

Delegation is *not* just giving someone else a job to do. Effective delegation means transferring to someone else the necessary responsibility and authority to achieve a particular outcome which will meet a part of the organization's purpose. Simply transferring one of your tasks or functions to someone else may well be better described as abdication rather than delegation. The reason is this. If that 'someone else' (the delegate) is to be able to meet the responsibility of achieving a professionally desirable outcome it is rarely going to be sufficient to say to him or her, 'There it is; that's your job now'. Even if he or she agrees with the intention, unless the task is an extremely simple and straightforward one the likely outcome of his or her endeavours will rarely satisfy either of you nor successfully meet the needs of the department, school or college.

In order truly to delegate to someone else what has to be transferred is *responsibility* (and necessary authority), not merely the labour involved; and the responsibility which should be transferred is for the *achievement* of the best possible outcome – not just the completion of a set of activities. For instance, if a head of a primary school wants someone else, say a deputy, to take over the school timetable, what is important, to both parties and to the school, is that the timetable which the deputy ultimately produces is the most effective one possible given the resources at the school's disposal. This is not likely to be achieved by the 'That's it; it's your job now!' approach if, for instance, the deputy has no previous experience of timetabling and little or no awareness of the head's expectations. Also, if the rest of the staff still think the head is responsible for timetabling, and the head has never before left this responsibility in anyone else's hands, other potential hazards to a successful outcome emerge. To be effective, delegation calls for much more thinking and planning:

- to define the desired outcome clearly
- to ensure that the delegate fully understands that outcome
- to check that the delegate has the necessary experience and ability to carry that responsibility
- to inform everyone else who may be involved/affected that the responsibility is being transferred and so give the delegate the necessary authority to meet it
- to prepare yourself for the consequences of the delegation.

Unless all these factors have been considered, planned for and acted upon, what transpires will not be delegation in any effective sense of that term; it may even amount to abdication. Giving someone a job to do without ensuring that they are properly prepared is tantamount to abdicating one's responsibility as a manager: in such cases instead of positively enabling a colleague you may be actively disabling them.

Accountability

At this point it is necessary to deal with the issue of accountability. Use of a phrase such as 'responsibility and authority' may, once again, lead to some confusion over precisely what it means in operational terms. Since delegation clearly refers to the *transferring* (of something) from one person to another, it is important to be absolutely clear from the outset what is transferred and what isn't. This is where the distinction between *responsibility* (accompanied by the necessary authority) and *accountability* must be plainly drawn. Since delegation involves a *transfer* of responsibility from one person to another, it cannot mean giving someone a responsibility which is already theirs. As a manager, it is a significant part of your responsibility to help those others, for whose work you have oversight, to meet their own responsibilities effectively. In doing this you are not delegating something to them. You are merely meeting *your* basic responsibility to them by offering them the support and supervision which ensures that your department, school or college meets its purposes. Delegation implies much more than this: delegation means that you are seeking to transfer to another something for which, until now, you have been directly responsible. But the painful fact about delegation which you have to accept as a manager is that, although you transfer a part of your responsibility for the achievement of a key part of the remit to another, *you remain accountable*. As the manager in one of the classic films illustrating the pitfalls and problems of delegation says to his personal guru, 'So if he gets it wrong I get the blame', and the answer of course has to be, 'Yes'. Accountability is not transferable; responsibility and authority are – and they must be transferred if delegation is to be effectively achieved.

Delegation and you

As a finale to this introductory chapter, it is useful to ask yourself how ready you believe you are to delegate to others. Although I hope I have already made clear some of the most essential elements of delegation, an important constituent in practising delegation is your own in-built attitude to your work. The short questionnaire which follows is designed to help you explore this. It does not pretend to be a precise measure. My suggestion is that you respond to it quickly at your first reading of it, giving your *instinctive* response to the twelve items rather than dwelling too long over them. Once you have scored the outcomes, you can then return to your individual responses and consider each or any of them more fully in the knowledge of the way they have affected your overall score. Achieving accurate self-assessment is never a precise science, and as this questionnaire seeks to help you uncover some of your basic, habitual reactions to work situations, it is best to try and record these first as a reflex action to the prompts provided by each of the 12 items in the questionnaire.

Your approach to work

Making an initial assessment

In the questionnaire below are 12 pairs of adjectives or descriptive phrases. Each of them relates to the way people behave/react in working situations.

Between each pair of words or phrases is a numerical scale which represents the continuum between the two behaviours which are being contrasted. For each particular continuum, circle the number which you believe most accurately represents your own behaviours. Do this in pencil so that if necessary you can make amendments later.

Complete the questionnaire quickly. You may, if you wish, test your initial assessment later, by observing your own preferred/instinctive behaviours as you go about your regular work over the next few days/weeks. If you do this, be prepared to amend your initial assessment in the light of any particularly strong indications which suggest to you a different rating for any item. Alternatively, you may wish to return to some of the items as soon as you have completed the scoring and interpretation steps which follow, and make some amendments to your initial responses: you can still check them against your own actual behaviours later.

(a)	Usually do things in lots of time	0 1 2 3 4 5 6 7 8 9 10	Don't mind working in a rush
(b)	Like to feel in control	0 1 2 3 4 5 6 7 8 9 10	Enjoy the unpredict-able
(c)	Impatient	0 1 2 3 4 5 6 7 8 9 10	Calm
(d)	Enjoy regular planned work	0 1 2 3 4 5 6 7 8 9 10	Like responding to crises
(e)	Accepting	0 1 2 3 4 5 6 7 8 9 10	Judgemental
(f)	Directive	0 1 2 3 4 5 6 7 8 9 10	Helpful
(g)	Listening	0 1 2 3 4 5 6 7 8 9 10	Telling
(h)	Doing today's job well	0 1 2 3 4 5 6 7 8 9 10	Thinking about where we'll be in five years
(i)	Easy-going	0 1 2 3 4 5 6 7 8 9 10	Always striving
(j)	Work to live	0 1 2 3 4 5 6 7 8 9 10	Live to work
(k)	Careful about details	0 1 2 3 4 5 6 7 8 9 10	Like speculating; seeing the big picture
(l)	Enjoy being in charge	0 1 2 3 4 5 6 7 8 9 10	Happy to be led

Scoring and interpreting your own assessment

Scoring

1. Add together the numbers you have circled for items (a), (d), (e), (g), (i), (j). Enter the result here: _____
2. Next add together the numbers you have circled for item (b), (c), (f), (h), (k), (l). Enter the result here: _____
3. Subtract this second total from 60 and enter the result here: _____
4. Now *add* the totals from 1 and 3 together
   Total: _____

Interpreting

If your total is 95 or more, it is likely that you will find it very difficult to delegate work to others. You may welcome their help but you will rarely leave anything significant entirely to them: you enjoy being at the helm, working flat out, seeing everything gets done correctly.

If your total is 70 to 94, you will probably find it somewhat easier to pass on responsibility to others – but probably for what you consider are the less important aspects of your work. You may also find that you just pass on the work involved rather than real responsibility for the outcomes, so that you find yourself checking on 'how things are going' or asking to be 'kept informed of progress' quite a lot.

If your total is 45 to 69, then it is likely that you will be much more ready to share your responsibilities with others, even to seek to do so and, at the lower end of this range, to actively enjoy doing so though without ever giving up final, overall control over what is done.

If your score is 20 to 44, you probably pass work on very readily to others and may have to watch whether you have always chosen the most appropriate aspects of your work to delegate. You may sometimes find you have in fact tried to hand over the job entirely. Check from time to time that you haven't simply doled out all the bits you don't like!

If your score is 19 or less, are you sure you really want to be a manager?

CHAPTER 2
Should I Consider Delegation?

Before considering the tactics and techniques of effective delegation, it is important to ask yourself the question 'Why should I?' If you completed the questionnaire at the end of Chapter 1 you may already feel you have begun to formulate a response to this question. Nevertheless, before proceeding further it is vital that you examine the fundamental convictions you hold about delegation.

In any form of human undertaking 'Why should I?' is a key question. Unless you, the undertaker (to give that word its less commonly used meaning!), believe that what you are proposing to do is worth doing, you are much less likely to see it through. Any lack of conviction will encourage you to seize on difficulties that emerge and use them as reasons for stopping altogether or accepting an outcome that falls well short of your original aspirations.

In the case of delegation, this normal human condition is emphatically underscored in two ways. The need for a secure fundamental conviction that what you are attempting is worth the time and effort involved is inevitably increased when the outcomes you are seeking are intrinsically difficult to achieve: 'pain often seems to outweigh gain'. If you are seeking to hand over responsibility and authority which is yours to someone else, the potential for 'pain' is high. If the steps which have to be taken to achieve effective delegation require considerably more conviction than the average to carry them through successfully, then further 'pain' may be anticipated and the sense of potential gain diminished. This is what faces anyone who seriously attempts delegation.

Furthermore, unless you are clear and convinced about the real benefit to you in letting someone else exercise a part of your responsibility on your behalf, *you should not attempt delegation.* This is because any lack of conviction will lead you to build in from the outset an *illusion* of the transfer of responsibility to some other person, with the reality being something very different, and sometimes very damaging to all concerned. I believe this is what occurred in the following situation involving an acquaintance of mine. A very experienced and successful headteacher of a reasonably sized comprehensive school was in the process of handing the school over to his successor (my acquaintance). He conducted the handover in a very thorough and professional manner. One small part of it concerned the role of the two deputies in relation to the report of the school's activities which was made to the governors each term. The retiring head informed his successor that this was a task he had 'delegated' to the deputies. He said, 'You don't have to worry about that. The deputies do it: the report is theirs, not mine. One of them reviews all the curriculum, teaching and learning side of the school and the other covers the pastoral and all the extra-curriculum and community stuff'.

When the new head actually started, she discovered that the first governors' meeting she would have to face was only five weeks into her first term. Remembering her predecessor's words, however, she did not worry about the reporting aspect of the meeting, even when the LEA sent her the outline agenda which included, 'Item 3: Headteacher's report', and asked for a copy of this to be sent to them ten days in advance of the meeting for circulation. She merely asked the deputies whether they knew of this deadline. Both replied they did and did not raise any other query. One day before the deadline, each deputy in turn arrived at the head's office and gave her a typed set of notes covering each of their respective areas. When the new head saw these she said, 'But

Mr Jenkinsop told me he left this report to you. Don't you actually produce the final report?' 'Oh no, not any more', was the reply from both of them. 'We did that once but he altered so much of it before sending it on that next time we just gave him lists of everything and he put those into in his own words'.

The point of the story is that *full, effective delegation* of the responsibility for the report to the governors had not actually been achieved. The deputies were involved and provided very useful assistance, but the report was still the head's, not theirs, as he had asserted. My informant (the new head) said she was convinced however that her predecessor *believed* that he had delegated the full responsibility for the termly report to the deputies. She said she found many similar examples in the school as she got to know it better. It was a very good school and extremely well-organized, but in almost every area the final decisions, and all the final actions associated with these, were in the hands of the head. That is not to say that schools or departments cannot be run in this way. They can, but what is happening in such circumstances cannot be described as *delegation*. Nevertheless, my informant, from her previous knowledge of the head, was convinced that he genuinely *intended* to delegate the full responsibility for the report to the deputies. And the 'damaging' part of this story? One aspect should be obvious already: everyone in that school was used to leaving everything, ultimately, to the head! Worse than this was the potential loss of confidence of the two deputies, caused by the loss of self-esteem arising from the dissonance between the previous head's words – 'I've delegated that: the report is yours now, not mine' – and his actions in rewriting the whole thing so that the report was, in the end, 'his'. So what had prevented the head in this story from achieving effective delegation?

I believe one key factor was that from the outset the departing head had never convinced himself that he should really leave this particular responsibility to the deputies. One obvious reason for that is the publicly exposed nature of this particular responsibility. It is at least arguable that he should never have thought of delegating this responsibility for that very reason. There are other possible, underlying reasons why his apparently genuine intention to do so was defeated by his lack of conviction. We shall return to those in a later chapter.

So, why should *you* delegate? Other aspects of the answer to this question are provided by the next two chapters; please proceed to those straight away if you wish. However, to remain for the moment at the level of your own broad, *instinctive convictions* about delegation, it may be helpful to ask yourself the questions below before moving on.

Should I consider delegation?

Questionnaire

Circle Y (yes) or N (no) for each of the questions below:

1. Do I often feel under pressure from the job?   Y   N

2. Am I able to give time, fairly regularly, to thinking about long-term plans?   Y   N

3. Do I often get interrupted by other people?   Y   N

4. Am I only really content in my job when I'm working flat out?   Y   N

5. Do I usually feel that a job has only been done well when I've done it myself?   Y   N

6. Am I surrounded by capable people who are only too ready to take on things?   Y   N

7. Do I find that I'm good at letting others take decisions for me on aspects of my job?   Y   N

8. Am I usually confident that I'm spending my time at work to best advantage?   Y   N

9. Am I usually on top of the 'paperwork' part of my job?   Y   N

10. Do I get worried if others in my department/ school don't tell me how things are going?   Y   N

Scoring

If you have circled Y for *any* of the items 1, 3, 4, 5 and 10, and N for *any* of the other five items, you should consider whether you can delegate some of your work. Each of these responses indicates that there is potential benefit for you in considering delegation.

If adding the number of Ys you have circled for items 1, 3, 4, 5 and 10 to the number of Ns you have circled for the other items produces an overall score of 7 or more, you certainly need to consider delegating one or more of your current responsibilities.

Scores of 3 to 7 still warrant careful investigation. Less than 3 and you are generally in control of your work: you stay on top of the job without too much pressure, enjoy the occasional slack period, and are surrounded by capable colleagues whom you trust to get on with things. However, check your responses to see that you really are behaving as you say you are: observe yourself in action using the items above as a kind of checklist. Even if this confirms your initial findings, there are other reasons why you might consider delegation further. All you have established so far is that your instinctive convictions about work do not cry out for you to consider delegation as an urgent priority for its own sake.

CHAPTER 3
The Benefits of Delegation

The pain/gain equation

This and the next chapter provide the basis for a more detailed response to the fundamental question posed in the previous one, by presenting the pros and cons for delegation – the benefits and the barriers. Further analysis of both sides of the pain/gain equation reveals that there are four main contributory factors which bear upon this equation in any management situation; these are:

❏ time
❏ pressure of work (in extreme cases, stress)
❏ control (and the related issue of status)
❏ the 'others' (with and through whom the manager works).

As in most human situations, these factors more often operate in interrelated ways than entirely discretely, so it is helpful to examine them from two different angles.

We will look first for an answer to the question, 'When to delegate?' by examining the reasons for or *benefits* to be derived from delegation. Following this we can quickly review (in Chapter 4) the same ground from the less positive – but very real – angle of the *barriers* to effective delegation, the 'So, what's stopping you?' question. By this means all four of the above contributors to the pain/gain equation will be addressed, though in different ways, representing the continual interplay of all of them in any real management situation.

Benefits of delegation

Time

One (possibly the most) frequently cited reason for considering delegation is lack of time: 'I haven't got enough time to do my job as well as I want to'. Alternatively, you may have heard, as I have, the comment, 'There aren't enough hours in the week'. This last observation provides a good introduction to two fundamental facts about time which are so simple and obvious that they are often ignored:

❏ there is never enough of it (however hard you work, 24 is the maximum number of hours in any day)
❏ you can't save it in the sense of keeping some of it back to use later, as you can with other kinds of resources.

From these two facts about time come two related consequences, the second of which provides one of the most fundamental benefits which can flow from effective delegation:

❏ you have to use time to best advantage; to organize it so that you apply the time that is available to greatest effect
❏ while effective delegation does not increase the total amount of time available, you can increase the proportion of time you have available for the crucial (contributing) parts of your job.

So delegation can help you meet the perennial problem of the lack of sufficient time to do the job as well as you would wish by providing a vehicle for the better deployment of the time which is available. This specific issue, and how you might plan to take advantage of it, is taken up again in Chapter 12.

Preoccupation

I am preoccupied by preoccupation. All my work with managers in many different kinds of organizations (and reflection on my own practice as a manager) convinces me that all of us suffer from the constant danger of becoming preoccupied with some aspects of our job to the exclusion of others, or if not exclusion, at least to the serious diminution of the attention we give to other parts of our role. In particular, we are all in constant danger of becoming so preoccupied by what we are doing (and all the things we believe we still have to do) that we cease to focus our attention sharply enough on what we are trying to achieve. I call this 'task domination': our natural desire to complete what we have set out to do comes to preoccupy us to such an extent that we lose sight of our overall purpose, our reason for doing it in the first place; we become obsessed with *doing*, as opposed to *achieving*.

To provide an illustration of this, I turn to the activity-based programmes I run on leadership. One of the team exercises involves each team and its leader in searching for a series of clues which will lead them to one final object. Teams receive points for each member actively involved in the search, and the discovery of each of the clues earns the team a further number of points. Discovery of the final object earns the team which finds it an even larger points bonus. Apart from the points awarded for discovery of the final object, each team competing in the exercise can, theoretically, earn the same number of points (the size of different teams being adjusted to allow for any advantage gained by having an extra team member). However, the *purpose* of the exercise, as set out clearly at the outset of the exercise is *to beat the other teams* in the competition: the winning team is the one with the largest number of points at the end of the exercise. The catch is that the exercise is also a timed one, and points are deducted from the score of each team for any time used after the initial start-up period. The exercise finishes either at the end of the total time allotted to it on the programme or, for any individual team, when it decides to signal completion by handing its own score of points, amassed up till then, to the tutor.

The crucial point in the exercise arrives when a team has discovered all its clues and is struggling to put together the information from them which will lead to discovery of the final object. This point is reached by almost all teams fairly quickly, and a calculation of their 'score' at that moment would reveal that if they hand in their score then, they may well maximize their total, rather than pressing on to try and find the final object while 'losing' points for each further minute they spend in this pursuit. It is of course a calculated risk because if another team finds the final object quickly, then that team's score will be higher. However, in only two instances of the dozens of teams I have now observed on this exercise have teams ever even paused to consider the possibility of stopping the search and handing in their accumulated points total: in one case they considered it and then decided to continue; in the other they stopped – and won because the only other team competing on that occasion pressed on, found the final object one minute before the programmed close of the exercise and lost (by 15 points) because they had taken so long to do so.

The point of this illustration is that in the case of every other team I have observed, they never even paused to think about the option offered to them by the way the exercise and its scoring system are constructed. In discussion afterwards, everyone has agreed, on every occasion, that the reason for this was because once the activity (of searching for clues and then for the final object) had begun, every team member became obsessed with the idea of *doing* her or his best for the team. So *finding* clues and the final object became their motivating force and they forgot the *purpose* of the exercise: preoccupation with doing obliterated the objective they were trying to achieve.

This observation is supported by the findings of others whose job takes them close to managers as they go about their work. One piece of research into managers' use of their time revealed, for instance, that although they can *do* a myriad of different *tasks* all at the same time, they are only really capable of giving *effective* attention to a maximum of five or six major areas of concern – the key objectives they are trying to achieve – at once. I believe that even within that small range, most of us become so preoccupied with one or two of these that we give much less attention to the others, certainly for significant periods of time, if not constantly. So, for instance, a head of department contemplating a major curriculum change may well forget for quite some time to check whether his or her department is carrying out agreed practice on the provision and marking of homework; this one certainly did once, with the result that the current generation of pupils were not so well served as they were entitled to be while I was obsessed with improving the lot of their peers in the future.

Yet all managers have to answer for the *overview* of the whole of their area of responsibility – the monitoring of its routines of operation and its continuous development. To do this a manager has to develop the capacity to direct his or her attention continuously to all the changing essentials of the job, rather than risk becoming too preoccupied with only one or two specific aspects of it. Delegation promotes this outcome by allowing managers to ensure that all key areas of the work are effectively covered by delegating some of them to others, thus allowing the managers themselves to focus on those which they decide require their personal attention.

Development of others

I hope it is apparent from what I wrote in Chapter 1 that I am unequivocally committed to the principle, first expressed in this form by the government's School Management Task Force in 1990, that anyone who accepts responsibility for the oversight and support of the work of others has to strive continuously to make it 'easier for them to succeed' and 'harder for them to fail'. It is a quintessential part of a manager's role to support the work of her or his colleagues continuously. One of the best ways to meet this particular responsibility is to look continually for ways of developing the skills and confidence of one's colleagues. This is very familiar ground these days; it is usually referred to as 'staff development' in any description of a manager's responsibilities.

However, more often than not, the traditional way of meeting this responsibility has been through one or other form of INSET: sending someone off on a course or organizing an INSET day for a group, or all, of the staff on a staff study day. More recently, a few examples have begun to emerge that a richer range of development opportunities is being deployed. Delegation is one way of providing this enriched range of support for the development of individual colleagues.

Delegation – of a part of *your* **responsibilities** – provides a very real opportunity for enhancing the growth of colleagues, especially where the part of your responsibility which is delegated is seen by all concerned as significant (as opposed to trivial). The anecdote quoted in Chapter 2 is – or could have been – an instance of this: giving a deputy the responsibility of compiling the main termly report on the school to the governors can hardly be classed as trivial. Empowering a colleague to decide for themselves and carry out anything which materially affects the way the department or school runs, or the way it is presented to others (such as governors or parents), will fall into this category: delegation of such responsibilities, if effectively carried through, is a rich source of development. Furthermore, this positive development of others also offers two other benefits: *cover* and *teamwork*.

Cover refers to the need for all managers to ensure that at least the main parts of their responsibility can be carried out by someone else in their absence. I would go further and argue that we all have a responsibility, if not to prepare our own direct successor, to prepare our organization for that succession. Working in schools in the 1960s and 1970s taught me to be somewhat leery of the 'departing charismat' who sets up brilliant new ideas and structures and then leaves before he or she has made sure that other colleagues are confident and knowledgeable enough in their use to ensure that work on them can be carried on successfully without him or her. Even without this particularly dramatic scenario, the idea of having others in your department/ school who can stand in for you on a routine basis when needed is sound practice: it provides them with developmental experience, you with a little more peace of mind and others with someone else to turn to in your absence.

Teamwork is currently an overworked word in management. Nevertheless its importance should not be ignored just because it has become somewhat hackneyed. Anthony Jay, writing about a specific piece of research into management teams some years ago, gave his article the title, 'No one's perfect but a team can be'. While not seeking to expand upon that headline in any detail, I do believe instinctively, with him, that a group of people working together is more likely to produce the best possible outcome than one person working alone. I certainly believe that the job of running schools is essentially one for teams of people rather than individuals. The inevitable ambiguity and complexity of much of the work done by schools convinces me that running a school or a department is not a single-person task. In this context, delegation to colleagues is one of the most effective ways to increase the sense of shared achievement on which all real teams thrive.

Reduction of pressure (and stress)

Finally, if even some of the above benefits can be brought to fruition, then clearly the sense of pressure which is a common feature of work as a manager will be diminished: you will be less likely to succumb to stress. To explain how this can come about I must explain how I have come to understand stress.

Here is my favourite (because it's the simplest I have ever encountered) conceptual model of stress:

In every aspect of our lives we are all continually called upon to meet demands placed on us (by ourselves and others) by deploying the resources we have at our disposal. Where these resources equal or exceed the demands, we cope – even though we may say (and feel) we are under pressure. Where the demands exceed our resources, stress occurs.

It seems to me that delegation which results in

❑ a more satisfactory distribution of one's time,
❑ an improvement in the focusing of one's preoccupations on the essentials of one's role,
❑ a development in the skills and confidence of one's colleagues, and
❑ an increase in the amount of genuine teamwork which comes through shared achievement,

clearly increases the resources available to meet the demands posed by the job of managing.

So how about it?

The questionnaire presented at the end of the last chapter clearly offers you one analysis of your current situation in relation to some of these potential benefits. An alternative approach, drawing more directly on the points made here, can be found below. If you wish to use it, it is best, once again, to react to each of the ten statements as *quickly* as possible. Then consider the overall level of possible gain you may obtain from delegation by joining together the points you have marked against each individual statement with a continuous line so as to provide a simple profile of your own current work situation. If you completed the questionnaire at the end of Chapter 2 it might be interesting to compare your 'score' from that with the profile derived from this exercise.

In order to gauge the possible benefits to ourselves, we need to review these in relation to our own current work situation.

Opposite each statement below, slash the line (representing the continuum between the extreme positions) in relation to the degree to which you think the statement applies to you.

	Does not apply	Does apply

1. I often work long hours and take work home

   ├──────────────────────────┤

2. I very rarely have time for family and friends during term time

   ├──────────────────────────┤

3. I have to spend too much of my time on fiddling routines rather than the important parts of my job

   ├──────────────────────────┤

4. I am unable to give as much attention as I should to the morale of my department/team

   ├──────────────────────────┤

5. If I want a job doing well I have to do it myself

   ├──────────────────────────┤

6. A lot of my work seems to have to be devoted to sorting out other people's problems

   ├──────────────────────────┤

7. I wish more of my colleagues would play a larger part in running our department/section of the school

   ├──────────────────────────┤

Does not apply   Does apply

8. I've tried giving
   other people jobs
   to do for me in
   the past but it
   hasn't worked

9. My colleagues are
   great people to
   work with but they
   seem to want me
   to take all the
   decisions for them

10. When I'm out of
    school for any
    reason there's
    no one to whom
    I can easily hand over
    my responsibilities

CHAPTER 4
What's Stopping You?

The barriers to effective delegation

The barriers to delegation all arise as a result of our perception of ourselves and others and the conclusions we draw from those perceptions. Whether these perceptions arise as a result of our in-built character traits or come about in response to accumulated experience, they lead to the formulation of attitudes which appear to us to be justifiably based on conviction. Instinctively we feel that we 'know' that the factors represented by these attitudes are 'true' and that, concomitantly, there is little that we can do about them.

It is in this way that they become potential barriers to our effective use of delegation. They are effectively the reverse or negative side of the same coin which we were addressing in the last chapter: they are the reasons why we should not – or more usually cannot – delegate. Notice that 'we' in the last sentence. Because these barriers arise from perceptions of ourselves and others, they present themselves in these personal terms: either 'we' can't or prefer not to, or 'they' can't or won't, do something. For this reason it is helpful to represent them as a comparative table headed 'Us' (the delegators) and 'Them' (the delegates); this can be found near the end of this chapter. Once again the coinage metaphor is helpful. In this instance you will see that each side of the coin is to a significant extent reflected by the other: each factor on one side of the table expresses or implies a corresponding difficulty or inability on the other. They are not quite mirror images nor exact opposites. Rather, it is the perceptions which give rise to the one which can, and often do, give rise to the other. So the instincts which lead us not to *trust* someone else with a responsibility we have been used to exercising may also lead us to explain to ourselves and others that the rational basis for our lack of trust is that they (the others) haven't got the *capability* needed to take over this responsibility. In this way we justify to ourselves, our decision not to hand it over – or sometimes our instinctive need to interfere in the actual execution of that responsibility when we believe we have handed it over, as was revealed in the earlier anecdote concerning the two deputies and the termly report to the governors. One of the hardest lessons to learn in delegation is that in handing over a part of your responsibility to someone else, you have to give them the right to do it less than perfectly or not quite as you would; in other words, the right to make a mistake. If we don't, or can't, it is counterproductive for both 'us' and 'them' to claim that we have delegated something to them.

Because the barriers to delegation come about as a result of two of the most fundamental factors which guide (drive) our own behaviour – our instincts and our experience – there is no obvious and easy way to deal with them. That's the bad news. However, the good news comes in two ways. Provided we become aware of these barriers and the potential pitfalls they pose in our attempts to delegate, there is a much greater chance that we will face up to them realistically. In some cases we may decide not to proceed with our intention to delegate, because we can't overcome the barrier; in others, having weighed all the factors carefully, we may choose the exact opposite course to that – as suggested above, choosing even to take the risk of a mistake being made – and trust our chosen delegate to find his or her way through and to learn from it.

The second piece of good news, as the later chapters will reveal, is that if we follow a planned approach to delegation we can greatly enhance our chances of dealing with the difficulties posed by each of the barriers, even probably remove some of them.

For the moment I suggest that it will be beneficial to spend a little time cementing your awareness of the barriers by considering each in turn in relation to your own current approach to, and experience of, working with and managing the work of other people.

The table below lists ten of the most common barriers which managers deploy, consciously or otherwise, to explain their failure to delegate effectively. It would be useful to discuss the list with a colleague, preferably a peer who has similar levels of responsibility to your own. If you know each other well, you may be able to help each other assess the extent to which any particular attitude forms a part of your own current armoury. The exercise works best if *both* parties are attempting to get a better purchase on their own instinctive approach to delegation.

If doing the exercise with a peer is not possible, select a colleague whom you find to be a good but active listener and, taking each pair of barriers in turn, describe to her or him where you think you stand in relation to that particular pair of factors/attitudes. A good, active listener will ask you open questions such as, 'What makes you say that?', or 'How do other people react when you do/say that?' Alternatively, she or he may ask you to tell her or him again what you meant by a certain statement about your own approach and then paraphrase what she or he believes you have just said or, later, summarize what appear to her or him to be the key points in your own description. Active listeners don't tell you what they are like in similar situations, or immediately leap to giving you advice; and only very sparingly do they use anecdotes from their own experience to illustrate a point about your situation. Consider sharing these tips on active listening with your colleague and, before launching into consideration of the lists of barriers and the extent to which any of them apply to you, spend a short time discussing the 'rules of engagement' which the tips imply.

BARRIERS TO DELEGATION

'Us'	'Them'
Trust	*Capability*
'I can do it better myself!' (ie, 'I don't trust anyone to achieve as good an outcome.')	'There's no one who can do it!'
Time	*Workload*
'I can do it quicker myself!'	'They've all got enough to do already!'
Enjoyment	*Willingness*
'But I like doing that: I'm quite good at it.'	'No one will want to take that on.'
Status	*Responsibility and pay*
'It's my job so I can't be seen to let someone else do it.'	'They wouldn't want to accept that responsibility: they see it as what I'm paid to do.'
Control	*Risk*
'I need to be sure that it's been done.'	'They'd forget or make too many mistakes.'

Clearly in every case it will be possible to demonstrate that there is some 'truth' behind the particular attitude. The point is that unless we begin to challenge ourselves over the number of times we instinctively raise any particular barrier, we will be unable to seek ways of overcoming it. For instance, saying there is no one capable of doing a particular task when they have never been given the chance to develop the awareness, skills and experience necessary, is bound to result in it being true to say 'I can do it better myself'. Similarly, if you have a genuine concern about (fear of?) losing control – and most of us have – then it is inevitable that your perception of the risks involved will be enormous.

So, if we have a serious wish to improve our levels of operation it is important to remain aware that one or more of these barriers may exist and that they can, if not openly admitted, diminish the likelihood of our achieving effective delegation.

CHAPTER 5
What Do You Think of it So Far?

This old by-line from the 1980s Morecambe and Wise television comedy series carries a serious message for all of us. There is always great value in pausing to reflect on what has gone before. It enables us to revisit and distil the most fundamental aspects of that preceding piece of learning or experience with greater clarity and precision. If we are successful in this, the understandings we draw from our reflection become more readily accessible to us: they are more available to us as parameters for the thinking that will guide our later actions.

This is therefore a particularly useful point at which to *stop and review* the key points about delegation that have been set out in the preface and the first four chapters. My experience of working with managers both *in situ* (ie, alongside them as they go about their routine tasks) and in training situations has shown me that the key to effective delegation, and ultimately to effective management overall, lies in our deepest convictions about ourselves, about other people and about the nature of work. It is these convictions, as I explained in Chapter 4, which bring about the perceptions (of ourselves and others at work) that we regard as the reality within which we have to manage. The perceptions in turn influence our decisions and, ultimately, guide our actions.

If I am correct in this assertion, then unless and until you are clear about the key elements that have to be present to make delegation an effective (rather than illusory) tactic of management, you are best advised not to proceed beyond this point. Furthermore, even if you are clear what those key elements are, unless you are also convinced that they are 'key' in my sense, then your further reading of this book will be desultory at best and further contemplation of delegation is at least inadvisable and at worst, potentially damaging, in terms of management effectiveness, for you and others.

You may feel both clear and convinced already, of course. If so, feel free to skip the remainder of the chapter and go on to the next. If, however, you are someone who, even despite a feeling of clarity and conviction about what has gone before, likes to pause and recapitulate things, then read on. I recommend a two-stage recapitulation process. The first is very simple and quick to complete; the second takes longer and requires more thought but has the effect of probing one's understandings and convictions at a much deeper level.

Recap – stage 1: eight key questions

Respond to each of the eight prompting questions below. Together they provide a short summary of the key points made in preceding chapters. Unless your response contains an emphatic negative to the first question, or a negative (or at best a half-hearted positive) to the majority of the others, then it is probably worth reading on: you have enough conviction and understanding to justify the expenditure of your time on reading the remaining text and possibly even testing out your further reactions in practice. Before doing that, however, stage 2 offers you a further opportunity to test out this current level of your comprehension and belief.

1. Does your job involve managing – supervising and supporting – the work of other adults (to distinguish this
   from the principal responsibility of every teacher to support and supervise the work of pupils)?
2. Do you wish to consider ways of meeting your responsibilities more effectively by delegating one or more of
   them to someone else?
3. Are you clear that even if you do this you will remain
   accountable for the outcomes achieved by that other person on your behalf?
4. Do you believe you can ever hand over part of your
   responsibility to someone else and then not interfere
   with the way they do it?
5. Do you find you don't have enough time for everything
   (job, family, friends, interests) you want to do?
6. Do you ever feel that you are not able to give sufficient
   time to the parts of your job which you consider are most
   important?
7. Do you want the colleagues with whom you directly work
   to have opportunities to grow and develop in their jobs?
8. Do you accept the need to trust people with whom you
   work even to the extent of trusting them to make mis-
   takes from time to time?

Recap – stage 2: critical incident analysis

What is called for here is a specific kind of reflection which is
usually referred to as 'critical incident analysis'.

First, select an actual experience of your own, the more
recent the better. It should be an experience which involved
an attempt to transfer responsibility for a task from one person to another.

Obviously it will be most beneficial if you were the person
attempting to make the transfer: however it is possible to
conduct the analysis on an experience in which you were the
intended recipient, or even an interested by-stander.

It does not matter how successful or otherwise you see the
outcomes as being. We tend to learn more easily from our

failures but learning from success, in the analytical way required, is both possible and advisable.

Next, replay the experience (the 'incident') in your mind – slowly, step by step as if you were reviewing an animated cartoon of the event one frame at a time rather than as a continuous film. Ask yourself questions such as:

❑ Where did this 'incident' actually have its origins? Who 'started' it? Why?
❑ Who did what first?
❑ How did the other person(s) involved react?

Repeat these questions, and questions like them, until you are satisfied you have recaptured everything which went on. It is helpful at this point to make brief notes of the sequence of events you have recalled. Use whatever format of notemaking you are most comfortable with: lists under different headings, continuous prose using your own shorthand, spidergrams, whatever.

Now look at the record you have made overall. Do any moments or events stand out as especially significant? Is there any pattern to the events, or between these events and others you recall (eg, 'X got angry', 'Well X always gets angry when she thinks I'm implying she hasn't enough to do.')

Finally, run through questions 2 to 8 in the list in stage 1 against the fruits of your analysis to check if it suggests any possible explanations for what occurred.

If it does, do these explanations seem to relate mainly to you or to the other person involved? If the answer is 'the other', be prepared to move on: we are going to consider 'them' in some detail. If the answer is yourself, what does that tell you about your current level of understanding and conviction about delegation?

If no possible explanations occur from laying seven of the eight key questions alongside your analysis, several possibilities emerge:

❑ You could repeat the check by utilizing the more detailed lists of reasons for, and barriers to, delegation from Chapters 3 and 4 and see if that throws up any useful insights.

❏ You can decide that the analysis is inconclusive and either repeat the exercise focusing on another 'critical incident' or return to the conclusion you drew from first asking yourself the eight key questions.

❏ You might ask how thoroughly you have managed to conduct your critical incident analysis: it is not a straightforward task for anyone other than the person who is possessed of strong natural reflective and analytical skills.

Final tip – don't agonize over this. When the whole recapitulation process begins to feel pointless, break off and decide where to go next, using 'hunch' as your guide if necessary.

CHAPTER 6

Where to Start?
Deciding What to Delegate

Three basic questions

In moving forward to the practical steps which must be taken to complete an effective act of delegation, it is instinctive to ask, 'Where should I start?' In the case of delegation, though the choice of starting point may well have a critical impact on the level of effectiveness achieved, there is no easy single answer to that question: the choice will be made in response to the reason one has for deciding to delegate that particular responsibility in the first place. However, it is useful to pinpoint that reason in conjunction with one's response to three other basic questions:

❏ What?
❏ Who?
❏ How?

In responding to each of them in turn, you are explicitly defining the stages through which the process of delegation has to pass if it is to be wholly effective. In other words, you have to be clear precisely what part of your responsibility you wish to delegate, to whom you wish to delegate it and how you should go about it.

However, lurking alongside each of these three questions is the fourth one – why? For instance, in order to be precisely clear in defining what you wish to delegate, you have to examine your reasoning in two ways: what you are aiming to achieve by the delegation and why that particular responsibility rather than another.

Why is also a relevant question in your selection of the intended delegate. If your whole reason for contemplating delegation is the development of a particular colleague, then the 'Why?' question will have been answered already by this stage. In all other situations it serves as a further check on the clarity of your intentions and therefore on the likelihood of successful delegation being achieved. In particular, it may well reveal whether your choice of a certain colleague has been guided by instinct more than rational analysis – of colleagues' workloads and existing experience, for instance.

Finally, it is often only possible to answer the question of how one should best go about delegating something by understanding the fundamental reasons for doing so. For example if, as suggested above, the choice of the delegate relates directly to a desire to extend that person's experience, then, by definition, their current lack of experience will play a part in determining the best method of delegation to adopt.

Thus asking yourself 'Why', frequently throughout the delegation process, is very important. However, responding to this particular question does not provide one of the distinctively separate stages in the process, which is the reason it is not included in the list of basic questions above. So, keeping in mind the 'Why?' question as a continual corollary to each of our other questions, let us now turn to each of the stages of delegation in turn.

Since a significant management skill is the ability to take effective decisions, each stage is best seen as an exercise in decision making, as follows:

❑ deciding *what* to delegate
❑ deciding on the person to *whom* you wish to delegate
❑ deciding *how* you might best go about achieving effective delegation – of the chosen responsibility to the person to whom it is to pass.

Consideration of each of these stages affects, and is affected by, each of the others. Each of them also involves several smaller steps, or considerations. None of these is complex in itself but attention must be paid to each in order to provide the best chance of succeeding; and because of the interrelationship of all three basic questions, it is necessary to constantly have each in mind even when actually working on one of the others. The sequence for completing the steps is not therefore always as linear as the layout above suggests. If the reason for delegating is primarily to provide an opportunity for the development of a colleague, then the 'what?' question is better answered second, for instance.

However, the original impulse to delegate comes most often from a consideration of one's own workload, and clearly you cannot answer the third question, 'how?', until you know exactly what it is you wish to delegate (and why) and to whom you wish to delegate it. So our starting point will be an analysis of the possible range of responses to the question, 'what?'. The 'who' and 'how' questions will be addressed in the next two chapters.

Deciding what to delegate

The first thing to do is to review your current work in some detail and see if any clear patterns emerge from which you can deduce some obvious conclusions about potential areas of your responsibility which you might delegate. An exercise to enable you to complete this process of review and analysis follows. It is important to read it through as a whole before starting on the first step.

This exercise is a practical analysis of just those parts of your work which are concerned with managing the work of others. Most managers in schools and colleges also continue to teach. This analysis is not directed towards any part of your work which relates to your own teaching.

Keep in mind any instincts or convictions about delegation (ie, giving someone else part of your *responsibility* while remaining *accountable* for the outcomes) of which you are

by now aware. Please read everything below before beginning.

Step 1: Three categories for analysis

Make brief notes, under each of the three categories for
analysis listed below, of everything you do in your job as
manager at present. Remember to omit all those tasks which
relate directly to your own classroom teaching (eg preparation and marking). Read all three categories before beginning.

Category 1: list first all the things you do which you consider *essential* to fulfilling your key responsibilities as head of school/department/deputy
head, etc.

Category 2: list all the other things which you, as head/
deputy, head of department, etc. *have* to do
currently (because if you did not do them no
one else would) but which you *don't* consider
central to fulfilment of your role as manager
of your school or department.

Category 3: list all those tasks you do, have accepted/taken
on, which are neither directed towards your
own work as a classroom teacher nor related
necessarily to your specific post as head/deputy,
head of department (ie, categories 1 and 2
above) but which you have taken on *as a result
of being part of the school's management
team.* Tasks such as organizing duty rotas or
helping with the timetable are possible examples of Category 3 tasks.

Note: Try to distinguish here between 'extras'
you do which you would do even if you were
still a main-scale teacher with no management
responsibility (eg, running the chess club) and
those extras you have taken on as an exten-
sion of your role as one of the school's managers (such as the examples quoted
immediately above).

Check: have you made a note of *everything* you do as a manager (ie, other than work related to your role as a classroom teacher) even if it is only a once-a-term or once-a-year task?

Step 2: Checking your own analysis

When you are convinced that you have recorded all the things you do in the management part of your job, look back first at the things you do which you consider are *central* to your role as manager (category 1).

What does this reveal about those aspects of your role which you consider 'key responsibilities'? Are you satisfied that each of these *is* a key responsibility? Does each of them make a contribution to the outcomes you believe you (and therefore your school/department/section/year group) are there to achieve? Is anything missing from this list? Are there any key responsibilities which have not been included; for instance in reviewing what you actually do, you may have not recorded a task which would lead to fulfilment of this responsibility because you just never find time to do it. Is there anything you want to add to this category (of essential tasks/key responsibilities) or anything you wish to transfer to category 2 or 3 because you now consider it less than essential in the sense implied here?

Now check the other two categories quickly. The distinction between these two categories is probably best measured by asking yourself what the reaction of others might be if any of them were not done at all. If the answer is, 'Oh, X is not doing everything she/he should', it's probably a category 2 item. If the reaction would be 'She/he's not doing as much as she/he used to do', it's possibly a category 3 item.

Step 3: Selecting possible areas for delegation

When you are as certain as you can be that you have categorized your work accurately, make an initial selection of some tasks/areas of responsibility you wish to consider for delegation to others. Highlight them on your own list in readiness for further analysis following reading of the next chapter. Don't choose more than four items from your list at this stage. Is it possible to include at least one from each category?

Note: this is not a final, definitive selection. Working through the remaining chapters might, quite properly, lead you to reconsider this step and start again from here.

Government health warning!

If your categories are right, the 'risk factor' (most usually indicated by fear of loss of personal control over an important aspect of your role) is highest in category 1 tasks, but don't let this stop you considering the possibility of delegating a task/responsibility from category 1. The potential *gain* – to you and to your colleague – is higher if the responsibility delegated makes a significant contribution to the key results areas of your job.

CHAPTER 7
Where Next? Deciding Who

Deciding on the person(s) to whom the responsibility may be delegated

From your analysis of your own work as a manager which you completed in the previous chapter, you should now have a list of three or four task responsibilities which you wish to consider delegating. If you haven't already made this initial selection, please do so now.

As signalled in Chapter 6, the next stage in this particular decision-making process is to decide on the person to whom you wish to delegate any one of these responsibilities. Because the decisions about what to delegate and to whom to delegate it are so interrelated, it is best to see this stage as confirming and clarifying your initial selection from your overall list of responsibilities. For this reason, it is advisable to complete the steps in the next exercise for all of your potential areas of delegation before deciding which of these you want to proceed with.

The pro forma for this exercise is straightforward enough and may be completed relatively quickly. However, before you begin I recommend reading the guidelines below. As with so much that has gone before, they are designed to help you retain the close link between your (real) intentions and the actions you may ultimately take.

Guidelines

Write in column 1 on the chart the preliminary list of those tasks you have decided you would like/wish to delegate. Then note in column 2 your initial response to the question 'why?' for each particular task/responsibility. Don't go on to column 3 yet.

Next, examine your own reasoning critically. Sometimes the first reason which comes to mind is not the real, or at least not the whole, reason. That is concealed by your apparently rational first choice. *Ask yourself 'why' several times.* For example, if you record as your first choice reason – 'To reduce the pressure on myself' – you could ask yourself, 'Why am I under pressure?' The answer to that might be, 'I have too much to do'. If you then ask, 'Why do I have too much to do?', a possible answer could be, 'Because I take on every new idea that comes up personally and people have come to rely on me doing just that'. So then the fuller version of the reason to record might be, 'To signal to other people that I am trying to pass some work on rather than take on any more myself – and so start to reduce the pressure on myself'. In other words, you will, if this were the case, have revealed to yourself that the real source of the pressure is a combination of your own personality and the reactions of others to that. That knowledge will give you a far better chance of succeeding with your intention to delegate.

When you are certain that you have identified in full your reasons for considering delegation in the case of each task in column 1, move on to column 3 and identify one (or more) colleague(s) to whom you think each of your identified tasks might be delegated.

The reason for identifying more than one potential delegate in any instance other than where the reason for delegating is 'to develop X' is this. Only further consideration of the validity of your choice in the light of the considerations which arise when you begin to plan *how* to delegate the responsibility will confirm who is likely to be the best delegate. This may be, for instance, either the one who has the most ready-made capacity for this task already or alternatively the one who stands to gain the most by the experience of taking it on.

When you have completed all three columns, check the outcome against the questions at the foot of the table.

DECIDING TO WHOM I SHOULD DELEGATE		
Column 1 Tasks/responsibilities to be delegated	**Column 2** Why? (Reasons for delegation)	**Column 3** To whom (Name(s) of possible delegates)

Questions

❏ Have you only delegated the 'dross' (the chores) of your job?

❏ Is there any task you have failed to delegate simply because you enjoy doing it?

❏ Has the person to whom you are considering delegating got time to do the task? If not, what can be done about this?

❏ If another member of your team had been making this selection, might it have been any different?

❏ Do you wish to amend anything?

CHAPTER 8
Deciding How to Delegate

Your choice of the most appropriate way to delegate any responsibility has ultimately to be determined in relation to each intended delegate. However, instead of starting this chapter where the last one left you, by considering your list of possible delegates, it is best now to stand back a little from the immediate realities of your own situation. This is to enable you to look first at the *principles* which should guide your choice of delegation method before moving to consideration of the specific individuals to whom you may finally wish to apply them.

The next three chapters are therefore devoted to this issue. This allows us to meet first the basic underlying concepts which bear upon the choice of any particular method of delegation (in this chapter and the next) before going on to look at a simple, rule of thumb approach to the application of these (in Chapter 10).

Basic concepts

In any act of delegation two key factors have to be borne in mind when deciding how to delegate; these are:

❑ the relative complexity of the task responsibility to be delegated

❑ the intended delegate's current experience and expertise.

Fortunately, in addressing these two factors we can call upon ideas derived from one of the most thorough pieces of research into the different ways of managing. In the 1960s two researchers, Paul Hersey and Kenneth H Blanchard, produced one of the fullest, most detailed studies of management ever recorded. Starting from the perspective of the behavioural approach to management, their researches led them to conclude that in any management situation three elements were constantly engaged in a complex interplay with each other. These were:

1. The needs of the task itself (eg, what has to be achieved, what resources are available, what techniques produce the best results, how these will be measured, and to what standards) determined, of course, by the degree of complexity involved in carrying out the task.
2. The personal/relationship needs of the individuals who have to carry out the task (eg, their need to feel confident, secure, knowledgeable about their own role and those of others with whom they worked).
3. The 'maturity' of the individuals who have to carry out the task, defined by reference to each individual in terms of the closeness of the match between them (their knowledge and experience) and each of the first two elements.

What Hersey and Blanchard revealed by their research is that the leader (or manager) in any situation has to select her or his behaviour so that it meets the needs expressed in the first two elements above. Put another way, what she or he does will always, inevitably, be a mix of actions necessary to see that the task itself is completed, and actions directed towards the needs of the individual who is carrying out the task. To be effective, a manager is always striving to get that 'mix' of behaviours right.

This is best demonstrated by regarding the range of possible behaviours (actions) open to a manager in each case as a continuum, the extremes of which are represented by the words 'high' and 'low', referring to the degree of detailed attention a manager will have to give to achieve the most effective results. Each of these continua is set out in this form below.

Task needs continuum

At the 'high' extreme of this continuum, the behaviours needed are characterized by full and detailed instruction both on *what* should be done to complete the task effectively, and *how*.

At the 'low' extreme, virtually no guidance on what or how is required: the manager simply needs to continue to make clear the standards by which the outcomes of the task will be judged (and in most cases even this is achieved implicitly because the manager's behaviour at the low extreme of this continuum is epitomized by the 'hands-off' approach). The continuum of manager behaviours to meet the needs of effective task completion can be represented thus:

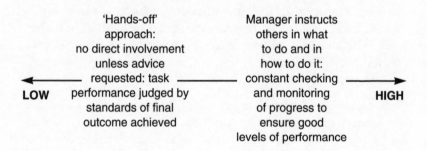

'Hands-off'
approach:
no direct involvement
unless advice
requested: task
LOW performance judged by
standards of final
outcome achieved

Manager instructs
others in what
to do and in
how to do it:
constant checking
and monitoring
of progress to
ensure good
levels of performance
HIGH

Personal/relationship needs continuum

In the case of the personal needs of the individual, the 'high' extreme of the continuum is represented by the regular personal involvement of the manager with the others, giving encouragement, supporting ideas, demonstrating by her or his visible presence that she or he values what they are doing and wishes to be seen to be a part of it her or himself. At the 'low' extreme of this continuum the manager still demonstrates warmth and support for the work of the others involved but much less overtly. Her or his support and confidence in the others involved is shown by letting them get on with it on their own while remaining interested in the outcomes and clearly grateful for their effort. The continuum of manager behaviours to meet personal/relationship needs can be shown thus:

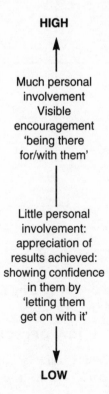

HIGH

Much personal
involvement
Visible
encouragement
'being there
for/with them'

Little personal
involvement:
appreciation of
results achieved:
showing confidence
in them by
'letting them
get on with it'

LOW

The balance of behaviours required when both task and personal needs are considered together

When intersected, these two continua produce this pattern of balanced choices between the two sets of behaviours:

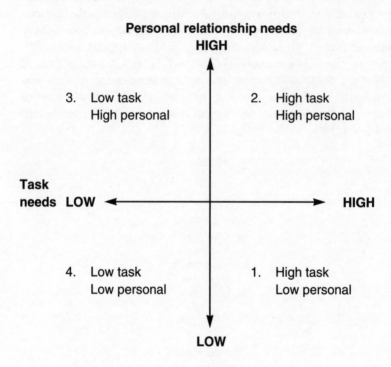

Personal relationship needs
HIGH

3. Low task
   High personal

2. High task
   High personal

Task needs **LOW** ←——————→ **HIGH**

4. Low task
   Low personal

1. High task
   Low personal

LOW

Hersey and Blanchard gave the following descriptions to this pattern of four different mixes of behaviour. The names used attempt to capture the distinguishing features of the balance of behaviours required in each case.

I. High task + low personal = telling

This combination of behaviours is characterised by a *one-way flow of communication* (from the manager to those carrying out the task), almost entirely concerned with how to do the task; hence 'telling'.

2. High task + high personal = selling

Here the introduction of overt, explicit concern for the personal needs of those carrying out the task leads to a blurring of the one-way communication flow which characterizes the 'telling' approach. Here the manager, in order to meet the personal needs (of greater involvement) of those carrying out the task, invites some response (questions/comments) while still ensuring that the main task directions are retained in her or his hands: hence she or he may be seen to be 'selling' the task to the others (ie, actively persuading them towards its completion).

3. Low task + high personal = participating

Now the balance of behaviours has shifted firmly in favour of the personal needs of those carrying out the task. The manager's concern for the task itself is reduced to retaining little more than the right to question (in extreme cases, veto) the mode of working chosen by the others. On the other hand her or his presence is still required to ensure that the task is effectively carried out because it serves the personal needs (of encouragement, support, etc.) of the other: hence the word 'participating' used to describe this approach.

4. Low task + low personal = delegating

Yes, we have arrived! Here the balance of the two aspects of manager behaviour is achieved by a 'hands-off' approach in relation both to personal and task needs. Any further attempt to give instruction, or anything more than an interest in how things are going and the final results, will be seen as unhelpful interference by those charged with carrying out the task. Hence the use of the word on which we have been focusing throughout this book – delegating – to describe this approach.

Further government health warning!

Hersey and Blanchard use the word 'style' alongside each of these four descriptors of the different points of balance between the two aspects of manager behaviour: this is what I was referring to in Chapter 1 when saying that delegation is used by some to denote a style of management rather than, as we are viewing it here, a tactic. I have used the word 'approach' because I wish to keep our attention on the essential elements of each situation rather than run the risk of simply adopting the four descriptors as 'style labels'. When this occurs the tendency is to assume two things, neither of which arise from Hersey and Blanchard's original thesis, and neither of which is borne out by my experience of actual management situations in schools, colleges or any other kind of organization.

The two fallacies are these: that the four 'styles' are discrete and separate and, more worryingly, that the adoption of any one of them in a particular situation is a fixed condition brought about by the level of adequacy (or more usually, inadequacy) of those others towards whom this style is adopted. So, a head misreading this thesis, might say of two heads of department, 'Now I know why I always have to tell John what to do: he's useless, whereas I know I can leave Joyce to get on with things because everything I've ever thrown at her she's coped with; she's a natural'.

The truth is of course that as the four approaches represent a balance created by two intersected *continua* of behaviours, there is nothing discrete about them. In fact the apparent lines between one approach and the next are in practice non-existent: the two sets of behaviours are constantly shifting, being adjusted to meet the needs of the situation. And the idea that any one colleague (or group of colleagues) is in a 'fixed state' and will always, forever and in every situation, require a 'telling' or 'selling' approach from the manager and never be able to respond to a 'delegating' or 'participating' approach, is as preposterous and fallacious as the assumption that pupil ability is a wholly immutable quotient fixed by the accident of birth and incapable of any development.

Deciding the best point of balance

This brings us to the central reason for presenting this thesis in this book. The key question which remains unanswered so far by my summary of Hersey and Blanchard's thesis is this:

What is it that helps us, as managers, decide which balance of behaviours (which of the four approaches) to adopt in any situation?

In the answer to that question lies the specific relevance of this important study of management approaches to our concern with delegation as a tactic of effective management. And that answer itself lies in the third element of the management equation which was Hersey and Blanchard's unique contribution to the study of management: the 'maturity' of the person(s) carrying out the task.

However, before going on to consider that aspect of their thesis (in Chapter 9), here are four short case studies to allow you to cement your understanding of the four approaches described above. Which approach is being described in each case? *Note:* 'answers' to these case studies may be found at the end of the book, if/when you require them.

Case studies

Case study I

A head is working with a small group of her heads of department who have been brought together as a working party to oversee the introduction of a new system of assessment to be used by all departments with Years 7 to 9. The group has only had one previous meeting and its chair is the most recently appointed head of department. The head is determined to ensure by her personal attendance at group meetings that the group does not lose sight of how important it is that every department fully comprehends the new system – the reasons for its inception and how it is to be applied to the grading of classwork and homework. The group includes the heads of the two largest departments, both of whom are long-serving members of the staff and very effective heads of their own departments. Despite her concerns regarding the importance of the task, the head does not therefore wish to appear to be trying to teach a senior relative how to draw the yolk from the products of a hen's labours.

What 'approach' is this head adopting in this situation with regard to her management of the chair of the group and the task of chairing the group she has given her?

Case study 2

A head of a junior school has just taken up his post. It is his first headship. Information gleaned by him in the weeks prior to his arrival has told him, amongst other things, that the first major school events in which he will have to play a part are the meetings with the pupils (and their parents) of the school's prospective new intake for next term. There are four local feeder infant schools, but his school has traditionally recruited from further afield too because of its popularity. He has also learned that the deputy head usually handles all the arrangements for these meetings, that they have gone well in previous years, and that the deputy head is regarded by everyone as very effective in her role and is a large part of the reason for the school's popularity (she did not apply for the headship). Having ascertained that she is happy to continue with this responsibility, the new head decides that the best thing he can do is to let her get on with it.

What approach to the deputy has this head decided to adopt in relation to the particular task of responsibility for the new intake meetings?

Case study 3

A head of an English department has a colleague who has been working with him for four years. Each year the colleague has shown increasing interest in helping with significant aspects of the running of the department. In particular, last year he stayed behind on several evenings to help in selecting new titles to be purchased by the department to extend its stock of literature texts. He displayed considerable knowledge of, and a penchant for, texts by newer authors, especially for use by younger pupils. This year the head of department decides to ask his colleague to take responsibility for seeing this task through, but says that he wants to see the final selection before the purchase orders are made out and that he is available to discuss any particular titles about which his colleague may have doubts. Which of Hersey and Blanchard's four approaches is this head of department adopting?

Case study 4

A head of a primary school wishes one of her curriculum coordinators to take over the role of mentor to the newly qualified teacher who is joining the staff next term. The head has acted as mentor herself up to now. The coordinator has no previous experience of the role of mentor and is completely unfamiliar with the new teacher competences emanating from the Teacher Training Agency. The head has therefore given the coordinator copies of these, together with her own notes on classroom observation and feedback and has arranged to see the coordinator after school, for one and a half hours on each of three evenings before the end of term. They have also arranged that once next term starts the coordinator will give the head a detailed description of what he has done each week for at least the first four weeks of the term. What approach is the head adopting towards the curriculum coordinator as he starts to undertake this new responsibility?

Reference

Management of Organisation Behaviour, Hersey, P and Blanchard, K, Prentice Hall, 1969.

CHAPTER 9

The Right Person for the Job: The Concept of Task Maturity

Task-specific maturity

This refers to the match between the intended delegate and the existing state of his or her readiness to accept responsibility for the task.

What Hersey and Blanchard discovered was missing from earlier attempts to model leadership and management behaviours was that part of the equation which relates directly to the capabilities of those others who are to carry out the task. As earlier chapters of this book have intimated, unless and until such people are fully capable of handling the task on their own, it is impossible to consider delegating to them the responsibility for doing so. In fact to attempt to (pretend to?) transfer responsibility to them before they have acquired this capability is, as we have seen, more akin to abdication of your own managerial responsibility than delegation.

So what is needed now is a greater understanding of what is meant by task-specific maturity and how it might be measured. Once these aspects have been clarified, we can consider in Chapter 10 some simple, rule-of-thumb steps you can take to actually delegate the task.

What does it mean?

Maturity, in this sense, is not seen as a general commodity or characteristic which one person may have and another hasn't. We may say of any colleague, 'She is very mature isn't she?', usually accompanied by the phrase, 'for her age'. Alternatively, we might observe, 'That kind of behaviour just shows how immature she can be'. In both these instances the quality of maturity is referred to as a general character trait. While this may have some bearing upon a person's task-specific maturity, Hersey and Blanchard were at pains to provide a much more precise interpretation.

First, maturity in this sense must be assessed directly in relation to the particular responsibility to be undertaken and the levels of specific skills and attributes required to meet that responsibility effectively: hence task-specific maturity. They go even further in pointing out that this often means that the use of job titles is misleading in this task-specific context. They quote the example of 'sales person'. If a person is given the responsibility of being a representative for a company and her job is to sell things, it is important to distil the constituent parts of that overall responsibility in order to establish her current level of relevant maturity. So, if she is a natural communicator who has been selling similar products for another company for five years, she is probably 'very mature' in this regard. If, however, the same person has a complete blind spot on the paperwork aspects of her role, so that although she obtains lots of orders from potential customers when she makes her first contact with them, few of these ever lead to a completed sale because she fails to fill out the requisitions to go to head office, then she is plainly 'immature' in this regard.

Thus task-specific maturity relates not only to each individual task responsibility but to the key constituent parts of that responsibility which have to be met if an effective outcome is to be achieved. Task-specific maturity measures the match between the skill/knowledge requirements of each aspect of the task responsibility to be delegated, and the existing level of the delegate's own competence/confidence.

How can we measure it?

The example of the sales person given above provides a clue to the more precise interpretation of maturity which Hersey and Blanchard put forward and on the basis of which they suggest the assessment of a person's readiness to take on a particular task responsibility should rest.

The simplest way to represent their conclusion is, they say, to see maturity as having two component parts: job maturity and psychological maturity.

Job maturity

This is much the more obvious element of the two. It refers to the knowledge and skills, acquired through education, training and/or experience, required to carry out the task effectively and to meet all parts of the responsibility adequately.

Persons with high job maturity will be able to carry out all aspects of the task without direction from others and they will be confident in their own ability to do that: they will see themselves as fully competent in the role assigned to them, and will be able to cope even if unexpected problems occur.

Psychological maturity

If job maturity relates to ability to do the task, psychological maturity refers to *willingness:* the motivation required to carry out the task. Both Hersey and Blanchard's original description and my own experience suggest that this element is best seen as being made up of two ingredients:

❑ *achievement motivation:* the capacity a person has to set her/himself 'high but obtainable' goals;
❑ *responsibility:* the desire a person has to take personal responsibility for her/his own work.

Measuring task-specific maturity therefore requires us to assess three things:

❑ the current levels of education and/or experience – job maturity – of the intended delegate

❑ her or his capacity to set her or his own goals – psychological maturity: achievement motivation

❑ her or his desire to take personal charge of her or his own work – psychological maturity: responsibility.

In practice, such assessment is probably best carried out consciously but informally, by observation of and reflection on the individuals concerned from the perspectives gained from the experience of working with them. The rule-of-thumb method suggested in the next chapter is one way of structuring this kind of 'conscious but informal' assessment.

Note: a third government health warning

The perspectives referred to above can only be gained by personal experience. This does not have to mean many years of working with someone. In some cases a few days of working together will suffice, especially if these are used deliberately to observe and reflect on these considerations. The judgement required should not be made simply on the basis of the written evidence provided by job applications and references: these may offer some insights which can be usefully followed up, but in the end there is no substitute here for personal experience.

Assessing task-specific maturity

A more formal way of making the assessment may be helpful, at least as a way of further clarifying the elements of job and psychological maturity so that the informal assessment recommended above may be more confidently concluded. I recommend the pro forma approach which follows, more for use in this way than as a precise tool of analysis. In other words, don't be suborned by numerical conclusions: still play your own hunch as well.

1. Think about both the intended delegate and the specific task responsibility you are considering delegating to him/her.
2. Have you analysed for yourself the main constituent

parts of that responsibility? For example, **the possible constituents of delegating the responsibility for next year's timetable would be:**

- technical know-how about timetabling
- knowledge of current timetable (pros and cons)
- awareness of any special requirements already agreed
- ability to talk to colleagues and negotiate with them when everything desired can't be achieved
- capacity for meeting deadlines.

3. When you have considered 1 and 2 above, respond to each of the prompts shown in 8 in turn, and slash the line representing the continuum between the extremes set out in each case.
4. When you have done this, relate the 'slashes' you have marked to the numerical scores at the foot of the table and add up the overall score which results from these.
5. Where any of your slash marks fall between two scores, use the lower score shown: this is because it is better at this stage to underestimate the maturity level than otherwise.
6. Finally consider the implications of your responses by reference to the table of totals (at the end of the list of prompts) and their accompanying suggestions.
7. Don't fail to play your own hunch as well at this stage. The reason for the recommendation to underestimate made in 5 is this. If you decide to act on your assessment, it is best when selecting the approach to be adopted to begin with a method which involves rather more task direction and less on the personal or relationship side than the reverse. Put crudely, it is much simpler to ease off from 'telling' someone what to do and how to do it and start to 'sell to' or even 'participate' with them, than it is to do the opposite.
8. **The prompts** (where X is your intended delegate):

Job maturity:

(a) X does not have the right
amount of education/
experience

X has all the
education/experience
needed

←————————————————————————→

(b) If difficulties occur, X
will not be able to sort
them out on her/his own

X is well able to
to meet any difficulties
which might occur

←————————————————————————→

Psychological maturity:

(c) X will need very close
support and supervision

X will get on very
happily on her/his own

←————————————————————————→

(d) X is usually reluctant
to take charge of her/his
own work

X is usually eager to
have a go for her/himself

←————————————————————————→

(e) X usually needs to be
reminded of the standards
we are trying to reach

X always wants to satisfy
her/himself that she/he
has done the best she/
he can

←————————————————————————→

(f) X often gives up when
snags occur or people don't
readily cooperate

X never gives up

←————————————————————————→

1	2	3	4	5	6	7	8

Interpretation

*Total scores
between*   *Interpretation*

42 – 48   This person is ready to take on the full responsibility now. Watch she/he doesn't take over your whole job!

30 – 41   Continue with your plans to delegate to this person but recognize that they will need you to stay in fairly close touch with them, offering personal support. See individual 'scores' to items (a) and (b) to see to what extent this personal support should relate to *how* to do the job or whether further training or demonstration could quickly give them the skill they need.

18 – 29   This person will need a lot of support and direction if the delegation is to be successful. Don't give up the idea but plan carefully how you, with your available time, are going to provide this. Almost certainly some (scores towards 40) or a lot (scores towards 24) of coaching will be needed.

6 – 17   These scores, certainly at the lower end, suggest that there is a mismatch between this person's maturity and the task you wish to delegate to them. Either a significant amount of further training and/or experience will be needed, or the level of task complexity must be reduced drastically if you are to achieve a successful delegation from this starting point.

CHAPTER 10
How Do I Go About It?

Having considered in some depth the principles which underpin the answer to the question first posed in Chapter 6 and repeated in the title of this chapter, we can now turn to the rule-of-thumb system I mentioned earlier. This is not meant to supplant the more detailed analysis provided in the previous chapter but it does offer a way to test out the conclusions you have now drawn from that and from your understanding of the central messages about task-specific maturity in Chapters 8 and 9.

Choosing a delegation method

The actual act of delegating can now be divided into two simple stages:

❑ *preparing* your colleague for the task responsibility she or he is to take on
❑ *supporting* her or him as they go about it.

In each of these stages it is worth considering four different, possible levels of preparation or support. This allows you to recognize that different colleagues will inevitably possess different levels of readiness for their new responsibility. Some of these will relate directly to the nature of the task ('task needs' in Hersey and Blanchard terms). The other aspects of readiness, as we have seen, relate as much to the personal needs of the individual concerned as to the task. The correct combination of one of the four different levels of preparation with one of the four levels of support will therefore reflect a balance between the task and personal needs of each particular situation.

The four levels of preparation

1. Summary briefing

Here your judgement is that the combination of the complexity of the responsibility and your colleague's job maturity suggest that all that is needed is a short, though clear, exposition of what she or he has to do, together with any important standards by which the outcomes will be judged.

2. Detailed explanation

Here you judge that a more detailed, perhaps step-by-step, exposition of each of the constituent aspects of the responsibility is needed. You will encourage your colleague to ask questions about anything she or he feels unsure about and check that she or he has understood and can do what is needed.

3. Demonstration

At this level, as well as the detailed explanation offered at level 2, you actually arrange a demonstration of the task and, where possible, provide your colleague with the opportunity to 'try it out'. For instance, if the responsibility is to take over the chairing of a working party you have been leading, you could invite your intended delegate to watch you do this at one or two meetings, handing over the chair for part of the agenda at the second to her or him. This level of preparation is usually required wherever what is to be achieved can only be really understood by 'showing': it is sometimes referred to as 'sitting next to Nelly'.

4. Formal training

Arranging for an intended delegate to attend a training course, on- or off-site, is obviously a good idea if:

(a) such a course exists or an internal scheme is possible, and

(b) it is likely to be effective in supplying your intended delegate with what she or he needs.

This is most likely when the 'deficit' you are seeking to remedy is one which relates to specific skills (eg, word processing) or knowledge (eg, a new exam board syllabus). Where the preparation required is directed more towards personal and interpersonal skills, formal training is less likely to be successful. More will be achieved by careful delineation (level 2) and possibly demonstration (level 3) of the task, followed by extra support, especially coaching where applicable. Nevertheless, such a programme of detailed preparation followed by continuing support through coaching might properly be described as formal training for this purpose.

The four levels of support

1. Monitor results

This lowest level of support requires only a formal check on the results achieved on completion. Many responsibilities in schools and colleges are of a continuing nature, so talking of 'on completion' may not seem immediately appropriate. For this very reason, if your assessment of your colleague's maturity suggests to you that you should let her or him get on with the task on their own, be careful to check that you have not, implicitly, given them *carte blanche* not only to meet the responsibility however they wish, but also to achieve nothing in particular by so doing.

Teaching as a profession is notoriously problematic in its approach to 'results checks'. This is not the place to rehearse the reasons for that or the importance, or otherwise, of the ambiguity it creates. What is crucial here is that in delegation, unless you create some means by which you and the delegate can estimate the level of effectiveness of her or his achievements, you are creating a potentially destructive vacuum for both of you. All of us need to have some benchmarks by which we can judge for ourselves what we have achieved (as opposed to what we have done: we're all *busy*, always, aren't we?). We also need to be able to explain those achievements to others from time to time, not least so that all the staff in a school can learn from each other and thus continuously improve and develop the level of their service to their pupils.

2. Guidance when asked

This second level of support represents a very small lift from the first. As the heading suggests, it still means letting your chosen delegate 'get on with it' on her or his own. However, in this case you make it clear that you are not only available to help if required but that you expect to be asked if any difficulties occur. Compared to the next level of support, the distinguishing feature is that you will not get involved unless you are asked. You will of course still check on the outcomes (as with level 1).

3. Interval checks

Here, because more support is required, you make it clear at the beginning that you will be occasionally checking on progress as she or he goes about her or his tasks. To develop the example quoted above in 'Demonstration', a head might, for instance, attend parts of future meetings if she or he decided to adopt this level of support. Once again, because of the peculiar nature of the profession, this kind of behaviour may not be seen as support at all, but interference. In that sense the example just given is not a very likely one. However, in the case of a new working party on an important aspect of the school's work, the head might clearly feel that it is not advisable simply to set the new chair (the delegate) in place and then withdraw and await the outcomes. An alternative form of 'interval check' might therefore be to arrange to see the delegate after some of the meetings and ask for a detailed account of how the meeting went and what is being achieved by the working party.

This level of support also includes a thorough review on completion rather than a simple 'check on results'. The earlier remarks on the need to define 'completion' apply with equal force here.

4. Close supervision

When this level of support is adopted, the manager is more or less present whenever the delegate is exercising that specific responsibility. Her or his presence is designed to help overcome difficulties which might be anticipated but cannot be precisely defined in advance. Clearly in exercising this level of support any manager will have to be extremely sensitive, particularly where the responsibility delegated involves work with others. It is very easy for 'close supervision' to become 'Stand aside, I'll do it'. For this reason, this level of support is often only used when the designed level of preparation cannot be applied, for example if the training is inappropriate or not available, or the complexity of the responsibility makes adequate demonstration difficult. It is important to be very clear with yourself that your *purpose* in being present is in this instance support, *not* demonstration or anything else, and to exhibit this distinction to the delegate and others by the way you conduct your part in the proceedings.

Choosing the best combination of preparation and support

Faced with any specific piece of delegation, it should now be possible to make an assessment of the degree of readiness of the intended delegate and, in relation to that, select an appropriate level of preparation together with the proper level of support.

So, if we take the example of a primary head wishing to delegate all the ordering, distribution and monitoring of stationery supplies to one of her staff, we might find this situation:

The colleague concerned is meticulous by nature, keen to help in whatever way she can, but very new to the school and the profession.

The head therefore decides to combine level 2 of preparation (a detailed briefing) with level 3 of support (guidance when asked). This will enable her to set out clearly what needs to be done and check that her colleague has understood, before leaving her to get on with it, while remaining overtly available to provide help whenever needed.

However, if an extra factor is in the head's mind, for instance a doubt about her colleague's maturity when put under pressure by old George who has been in the school 28 years and always says he has run out of paper, then the level of support might be beneficially raised to 3 (interval checks).

Finally, it is of course perfectly possible, and often advisable, to choose one level at the outset of an act of delegation and change to another (usually a lower one) fairly soon afterwards. In other words, the initial choice of levels of preparation and support is only ever a preliminary one to be reviewed in the light of the actual circumstances which occur once delegation has begun. Clearly this is more likely to apply to the level of support chosen, though even in the case of preparation some change may be called for. This in turn refers to the point made in the last chapter about erring on the side of underestimating levels of maturity and so overestimating the levels of support (and possibly of preparation) required. It is always easier to 'take the hands off' and lower one's involvement when you can see the need, rather than, for example, to try and impose interval checks on someone to whom, up to now, you have only been offering advice when asked.

Summary

As an extra check at this crucial stage, when you are about to launch yourself (and a colleague) onto the potentially fearful 'Sea of Delegation', here is a simple summary of the key factors involved.

To decide which combination of the levels of preparation and support are required to delegate any particular task effectively, consider these four factors:

Task complexity:

How difficult is it to grasp this task and to carry out the required responsibility well?

Task significance:

How important is the contribution this task makes to the school's overall effectiveness and its further development, ie, what's the 'cost' if it's not done well?

Colleague ability:
(Job maturity)

How much previous experience or training in this task does your colleague have? How confident is she or he in her or his skills/knowledge of this task?

Colleague commitment:
(Psychological maturity)

How keen is your colleague to take on this responsibility? Does she or he really want to achieve what you (the school) needs to be achieved from this task?

CHAPTER 11
Trying It Out

Case studies in choosing a delegation method

The first part of this chapter is a series of five case study situations, all of which are derived from school settings.

There are no perfectly correct answers to these situations. They are included here to enable you to try out your own interpretation of my suggested rule-of-thumb method in the previous chapter before going on to plan the actual delegation of some of your own responsibilities. You will find my recommended pairings of the two levels – of preparation and support – at the end of the chapter.

Read each case study in turn and then record your initial assessment of the levels of preparation and support required by writing the numbers of each level in the box provided at the end. Then, if you wish, compare your assessments with mine.

Here is a summary of the different levels:

Preparation	*Support*
P1 Summary briefing	S1 Monitor results
P2 Detailed explanation	S2 Guidance when asked
P3 Demonstration	S3 Interval checks
P4 Formal training	S4 Close supervision

Case study 1

A head has been attending monthly meetings of a group of heads of departments to monitor progress in planning the implementation of some major changes in the school's curriculum. Now the initial negotiations are complete, she wishes to delegate this task to the senior teacher who coordinates timetabling procedures. She wants the senior teacher to listen to the discussions, report progress and raise any problems which arise at the weekly meeting of the senior team. The senior teacher has never been a head of department and has only previously attended meetings of heads of department in company with the rest of the senior team.

P	S	

Case study 2

A head of a large primary school has a secretarial assistant who also acts as telephone receptionist. The assistant currently passes every call on to the head unless the caller specifically asks for someone else. The head wants the assistant in future to ascertain, where possible, the nature of each call and direct it to the most appropriate member of staff if they are free, or take a message for that person to return the call later. The assistant has a naturally good manner on the phone and had experience of telephone reception duties in her previous job.

P	S	

Case study 3

One of the major departments in a very large (1800+) secondary school needs to make major changes in both the content of its courses and the styles of teaching and learning used. At present students are at best apathetic about the subject, which has very low take-up in the sixth form, and has produced no applicants for study in higher education for the last seven years. Staff in the department know the changes are in train and broadly what form they will take. The head now wants to delegate to the head of department the responsibility for implementing the agreed changes.

The head of department is new to the school, and relatively inexperienced in handling people, but very knowledgeable and experienced in her subject, full of enthusiasm and keen to get on with the introduction of the changes.

P	S

Case study 4

A deputy head in a primary school, who is experienced in both budgeting and timetabling, has been asked by her headteacher to prepare a detailed budget of the staffing requirements and material resources needed to introduce specialist teaching of the National Curriculum (Key Stage 2) science to years 4, 5 and 6 in her school. The school already has specialist accommodation adequate for the purpose.

A week following his request to the deputy, the head is taken seriously ill and the deputy is made acting head. She now wishes to delegate the responsibility for drawing up this budget to the teacher who is the curriculum coordinator for science. This teacher is an experienced colleague and a competent science specialist. She has never been asked to do a task like this before as the school has until now relied on each of its class teachers to cover the science required by the National Curriculum.

P	S

Case study 5

A recently appointed head of department wants to develop one of her colleagues who is very competent in her basic work but seems to have lost a lot of her earlier enthusiasm; she has been in the school a long time. The colleague is an instinctively good and logical organizer and has proved over the years that she exercises sound judgement both in her selection of resources to use with her classes and in the methods she uses to deploy them to best effect for the pupils' learning.

The department would benefit from a complete audit of all its text books and other learning resources, including audio-video equipment and tapes. No existing stock records can be found, though the resources are generally well organized and tidily kept in the various stock cupboards used by the department. The head of department decides to ask her experienced colleague to take on this task.

P	S

Planning to delegate some of your own responsibilities

You may now feel ready to start making plans actually to delegate one or more of your current responsibilities to a colleague.

Return to the chart you completed at the end of Chapter 7 and see the comments in the guidelines relating to column 3. In the light of your fuller understanding of the processes involved in choosing a delegation method related to the maturity (or readiness) of the intended delegate, check whether you wish to amend any part of that chart.

The various checks

❑ Bearing in mind the task complexity and importance, have you chosen the right person to whom to delegate this task?

❑ Are your reasons for delegating this responsibility still sound?

❑ Is this the best/right task to choose to delegate?

❑ Is there another task which might give you a better chance to test out the various steps you need to take if you are to achieve effective delegation?

Note: on this last point, be as ambitious in your intentions as you feel you can be, but don't miss an opportunity to try out your skills as a delegater on an apparently more straightforward situation before 'going for gold'.

Action planning

Once you have made the checks to your own satisfaction, you need a written plan of action.

Interestingly for a profession which deals so much with the written word, teachers, in my experience, often seem notoriously reluctant to take this step of committing their plans to writing in a structured form. Is it because it is seen, once again, as likely to interfere with the intuitive; to reduce art to something more like science – or even, heaven forfend, to something more like 'business'? I don't know the answer. I do know that if you can bring yourself to prepare a written plan of action the likelihood of your being successful will be greatly enhanced. In working with many managers in schools and colleges I have found that not only do those who prepare a written plan generally meet more of their own original intentions than those who don't, but that they do so even though they frequently amend, or even entirely replace, the original plan. Somehow writing it down aids clarity at the outset, offers benchmarks on progress and provides an 'incentive to continue' which the apparent flexibility offered by carrying your plans in your head does not. Having a written plan does not mean you have to make irrevocable, inflexible choices. It is actually easier to amend a written plan which spells out things like 'reasons' and 'deadlines': if circumstances affect these, the plan can be altered relatively easy because the effect of changing one aspect can be traced through the rest of the plan.

A delegation chart

I have provided an outline of a possible action plan in the form of the 'Delegation chart', below.

There is nothing magical or precise about this particular chart. You may find one or other of the exercises in earlier chapters gives you a better format for your purposes. Throughout this book I hope that I have made clear how vital it is that you believe (and trust) in the steps you decide to take. Be prepared therefore to adapt the attached chart to suit your needs or draw up a completely different one if you prefer. But do draw up some form of written plan: it will provide some much-needed support for your progress towards effective delegation, I promise!

DELEGATION CHART

Task responsibilities to be delegated	Name of delegate	Reason for delegation	Initial estimate of delegate's readiness (P and S)	Amount/type of training and/or support needed	When by? (Deadlines?)	Date(s) for checking progress and 'result'

'Answers' to the five case studies

Case study 1

My starting point in this situation would be P3/S2. Given the implicit sensitivity of the process and the senior teacher's lack of direct experience of this particular role, it is probably best for the head to 'model' the required style of chairing which she sees as vital and then stand well back unless asked for help.

Case study 2

Here I suggest P2/S1. A detailed explanation of the head's need for the secretarial assistant to take over responsibility for routing the calls is probably required (rather than the summary briefing implicit in P1). However, the nature of the situation will provide its own checks, so S1 will allow the head to stand back and trust the secretarial assistant to get on with it, knowing she can return to further explanation/coaching if the results are not 100 per cent right from the beginning.

Case study 3

Unless I had personal knowledge of a very effective training course in the management and leadership of people through periods of critical change, I would recommend a P2/S4 approach to this situation, with the S4 becoming S3 as soon as possible. The changes required are 'major' – they cannot be put off. The department is a large one and the head of department's 'unreadiness' lies only in the 'people' aspects of the situation.

If effective training were available then, P4/S3 would be my starting point.

Case study 4

Here I would select a P2/S3 balance. The curriculum co-ordinator is competent (technically in terms of science) and experienced in the school (ie, knows colleagues and systems) but this is an entirely new task, one in which there are no models from previous years on which to rely. It is not really susceptible to full demonstration, or training, therefore P2. However, both its importance and the need to ensure its effective completion, without any previous pattern to follow, suggest to me that S4 or S3 is required. S4, in the circumstances of this case, would mean the deputy had in fact hardly gained any personal relief from the delegation, so I chose S3. As soon as this level of support appears to be working, S3 could become S2.

Case study 5

Here the beneficiaries of a successful delegation will include the delegate, head of department and the department itself. Since a prime objective is the rekindling of an experienced colleague's enthusiasm, care must be taken not to choose methods of preparation and support which suggest incompetence, the need for radical retraining or close supervision. Yet the importance of the task in the eyes of the delegate is a key to success too. I would therefore choose to start with P2 and in the light of the experienced colleague's immediate reaction to the brief being provided by P2, I would select either S2 or, if she was very positive, S1.

CHAPTER 12
Time to Delegate?

No, the title to this chapter is not an exhortation to 'get on with it'. It refers of course to the whole issue of time which was touched on very briefly earlier. At that point (Chapter 3) I was first making the point that a more effective use of your time as a manager is potentially one of the most important benefits to be gained by delegation; and later (Chapter 4) we met time as one of the possible barriers to effective delegation. I think it is important at this final stage to revisit the issue of time, on two levels – first the general, 'More time not less' and then the specific, 'Analysing your use of your management time'.

More time not less?

At the start of this book, because I did not wish to risk interrupting the flow of narrative about the process of delegation, I deliberately refrained from admitting that *at the outset* of any progress towards delegation the time factor is a negative not a positive one. In this sense, as one begins any process of delegation, the phrase, 'I can do it quicker myself', is absolutely true. You cannot undertake all the key steps recommended in the previous chapters without expending more of your own time initially. That's the bad news.

Even worse is the news that, given that initial extra expenditure of time (and the concomitant extra focus on or preoccupation with developing your plans towards delegation), it is highly likely that your overall effectiveness will go down. However, the very good news is that this situation is not only a temporary one, but as the earlier claims about 'time' as a potential benefit suggested, as the initial extra expenditure of time diminishes so the level of effectiveness rises. The now positive gap between the two continues to widen, provided you have followed and continue to follow, the steps which can lead to the *realities* of delegation that have been presented here rather than some of the possible illusions which we considered earlier.

I am indebted to a colleague of mine, David Casey, for an idea for a diagram that usefully illustrates this point.

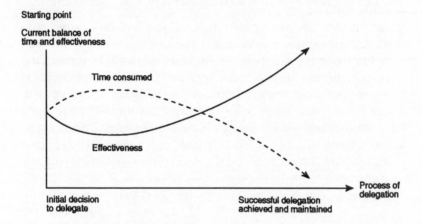

Starting point

Current balance of time and effectiveness

Time consumed

Effectiveness

Initial decision to delegate

Successful delegation achieved and maintained

Process of delegation

Analysing your use of your management time

On the issue of time, I believe it will be helpful to provide you with one of the most useful (because it is one of the simplest) analyses of management time which I have ever come across. In my training work with managers and management teams I use it constantly, alongside the ideas on delegation presented in this book.

If you find it of interest and you wish to make actual use of it as an analysis of your own management time, you will have to complete a log of your own use of your management time over, say, three or four days. These need not be consecutive days and you will benefit most if you choose to keep this record of your management time on the days when, for instance, because you have your lowest teaching load, you expect to be carrying out a lot of your management tasks. The chart you completed at the end of Chapter 6 may be a help in selecting the best days.

Keeping a log of your management time

To complete such a log you need to be meticulous about recording every separate activity and timing it. For example:

You are in the staff room at 8.15 am, writing a note to a colleague whom you may not see until the end of the day, asking her to see you, at the end of tonight's meeting, about the test procedures you are both involved in next week (and for which you are responsible). Before you have completed the note, another member of your team comes in and asks if he can have a quick word. Some minutes later, after you have talked, you return to the note only to be interrupted by the staffroom telephone ringing. As no-one else is present you answer it. It is for a colleague but as it is a parent whose child is having some difficulties at present, you take the message and agree to ask the colleague to return the call as soon as possible. You write a brief note to that effect and put it in your colleague's pigeon-hole. By now it is time to go and register your class, so you quickly finish the original note and leave the staffroom. On the way to your class the caretaker stops you to ask you about the arrangements you require for your meeting with staff and parents at the end of school today.

To be effective as an analysis of your own use of time, employing the categories of management time set out below, each of the individual activities which make up the situation above requires logging and timing separately, namely:

- writing your note to your colleague
- talking to the other colleague
- answering the parent and writing the note about that
- returning to the task of finishing the original note
- moving to your classroom for registration
- talking to the caretaker (even if only to arrange to see him later).

Keeping a log of this kind is itself a demanding task and for this reason also it is best not to try and do it across several consecutive days. If, however, you do manage to capture at least three or four days' worth of your use of time in this detail (across, say, two to three weeks of your work), analysing this log against the categories below can be very revealing: more of that later (see page 79, Completing the analysis of your own use of time).

Five key categories of management activity

- ❏ PLANNING
- ❏ ADMINISTERING
- ❏ LEADING
- ❏ CHECKING (OR MONITORING)
- ❏ REPRESENTING.

The idea behind this list is that in order to manage effectively, any manager with significant personal responsibility for the work of a group of colleagues will have to give some personal attention and therefore time to each of them, as follows.

Planning   refers here specifically to long-term thinking about the future and any steps required to investigate/research possible alternatives. It does not refer to planning next term's report procedures, for instance. Although the word 'planning' might well be used in this

instance, such an activity would be categorized here under administering (see below).

Administering refers to all those tasks required to ensure
that routine and immediate (short- and
medium-term) arrangements are in place.

The distinction between these two categories is that once any system or procedure
has been made a part of the school's systems, carrying it out – even if that means
planning a long way ahead – should be clas-
sified as administration.

Planning as used here refers to the more
speculative thinking-about and investigating
the future, so considering possibly better
ways to complete reports in the future or
researching alternative formats for reports
would be planning in this sense, whereas
preparing for the actual procedures themselves is classed as administering.

Leading as used here, refers to *any* activity which
relates directly to the *people* side of the job
of management, so encouraging, motivating,
criticizing, supporting, giving advice or guidance to individuals or groups will fall into
this category.

**Checking
(or
monitoring)** refers to those tasks of management which
have to be carried out to ensure that what it
was decided to do has been done, and done
properly. Hence the alternative word, monitoring – seeing that we are doing what we
said we would do.

*It may be helpful here to present the
three-form typology of reviewing, monitoring and evaluation which I met during my
time working with the old School of
Education at Sussex University. There they
used reviewing to mean simply replaying
and recording what has occurred.*

*Monitoring they defined as above to mean
checking what has been reviewed against
the original intentions of those involved,
and evaluation concerns, as the word
implies, the ascribing of value to what has
been done. These three processes can be
seen in action in the following exchange:*

*'Yes we did that'.
'And we did it precisely as we said we
would!'
'Yes, but was it worth doing?'*

Checking as used here covers the first of
these two activities: evaluation, asking the
question 'Is it worth doing?', would be better categorized here under 'Planning'. It is
an essential, but not so regular, activity
which implicitly looks to the future by rais-
ing key questions about the present.

Representing refers to those activities of management
which are concerned with representing your
department, team, section of the school, etc.
to others. So, attending a meeting with
other curriculum coordinators, heads of
department, heads of year inside the school,
or meeting parents, governors, employers,
the local community and talking about your
particular area of management responsibility, are all acts of 'representing' in this sense.

Completing the analysis of your own use of time

Now to return to your own time-log. If you have managed to
record a significant amount of data (one day's worth of time
is clearly not enough for this purpose) the next step is to
check each separate activity against the five categories above

and, by using the initial letter (P, A, L, C or R) of each, analyse your own use of your time.

Note: it is probable that you will feel that some activities might be placed in more than one of the five categories. For instance, you may be meeting with a newly qualified teacher who has just joined your team in order to *check* that he has understood and is properly following the procedures for the setting and marking of homework. If this is the first time you have made this check, it will be important that the way you do it does not demotivate your NQT colleague by making him feel incompetent or threatened. In adopting a purposeful but light touch approach, asking open questions and offering immediate help with any difficulties which appear, you will be consciously using this same occasion to *lead* and *guide* your colleague. Hence the time given to this meeting would require both C and L to be recorded against it. However, since we are going on to add up the total amount of time you spend on each category, you have to guesstimate the proportion of time given to C and to L. If 30 minutes was the overall time taken for the activity described above, you might decide that although your primary purpose was to *check* homework procedures, the newness of your colleague meant that you gave significantly more time to the 'leading' aspects on this occasion than you might at some other stage so C(10), L(20) might be your conclusion.

You may also come across an activity which does not seem to you to fit into any one of the five categories. If so mark it 'O' – meaning 'other'. Remember that any teaching, preparation or marking of work for your own pupils should be *excluded* from this analysis entirely. They should not be simply classed as 'O' activities because this will affect your 'averages' (see below). However, you may feel that some of your management work should receive an 'O' because it does not meet the specifications or descriptions given to any of the five categories above, for example tasks which fall into category 3 on your chart in Chapter 6. This is fine; don't *force* all your work into one of these five categories. If you don't think any particular activity you have logged properly matches any of the five specifications, classify it as an 'O'.

You are now ready to complete the analysis. Add up the amount of time recorded for each of the five categories and for all 'O' activities. Then add all these six sub-totals together to give you the total amount of time recorded against all your logged activities for the number of days you kept the log. That final total is your 100 per cent for the purposes of this analysis.

Convert each of your six sub-totals into a percentage of that overall total. To the nearest whole number is sufficiently accurate for this purpose but, if your arithmetic is anything like mine, check at the end that the six percentages you arrive at do add up to around one hundred!

Interpreting the analysis

The first question to ask yourself now is whether you are satisfied with the proportion of time you appear to spend on each of the categories: do you feel the balance between the various categories is appropriate for your job? Do you feel, for instance, that you do enough leading, or too much administering, or not enough planning etc., in relation to the percentage of time you give to the other categories?

The reason for asking yourself this question *first* is that there are some indicators available to us from others – researchers and consultants in the use of management time – on the most effective balance for managers who have overall responsibility for the work of groups of other colleagues. Heads of department and headteachers certainly fit the model of manager these researchers were studying. Here are their findings:

Category of Activity	Percentage of Manager time
Planning	around 10%
Administering	not more than 25%
Leading	at least 40%
Checking	not less than 15%
Representing	not more than 15%
Other	0%

You will have noticed that the overall total of the percentages above is more than 100. This is not a mistake; the figures are indicators not absolutes. They were arrived at by observing large numbers of managers at work, noting how they disposed of their time, and what balance between the five categories appeared to produce the most effective outcomes.

I offer you these findings here because it seems to me that they carry important messages for all of us as we consider using delegation as a part of our management armoury. By way of illustration I give below the figures from my own first use of this analysis and the key messages I picked up from them in reference to my own dispositions of time then. At the time I was the head of a comprehensive school.

Planning – 1%
Administering – 35%
Leading – 24%
Checking – 0%
Representing – 24%
Other – 16%

My first immediate, astounded reaction to these figures was, 'But I do plan and check; this is ridiculous'. It wasn't.

Whatever I might have felt about the precise numbers which emerged for each of the categories, I had to accept that over the period of time in which I recorded and timed my various activities, I had done no monitoring, very little evaluation (and therefore little thinking about the long-term future), and too much administration. I was probably aware of the latter before I did this analysis but the former two conclusions surprised me. The lack of any regular monitoring activity on my part was confirmed when I reviewed the general pattern of my work over the previous two years.

Whatever else, the analysis and these indicators made me think. Returning to them many times since, I find they contain important messages:

Beware of spending *too little* time on supporting and guiding (ie, 'leading') the people with whom you are working: you need to spend nearly half of your time on that. Don't confuse *administration* with management – 'pushing the paper around' has to be done, but it should be one quarter of the job at the most. Be careful that *representing* your department/school to others doesn't become an attractive substitute for working out solutions and improvements on the job itself. You need to be around for the latter, so 20 per cent is an absolute maximum for representing. To work out solutions and improvements, you must regularly *monitor* what's going on, and from time to time, stop, ask yourself if it is worth doing that, and if so if there is a better way to do it in the future, and think about what it all might look like in a few years' time, in other words: *plan*.

And the 'O' = 0 per cent message? Don't spend any of your management time on things which can be just as effectively done by others, unless you have to – for instance, if there is no one else to whom you can delegate some of the excessive administration you find you have to do.

Typicality

Finally, it will be very surprising if by now you haven't said to yourself something like 'But the days I recorded weren't typical. On other days I'd probably spend a lot of time on leading and not have my 88 per cent score on administering!' Well yes, there will be some truth in that reflection, but ask yourself as objectively as you can how closely the pattern of percentages revealed by your analysis reflects the general pattern of your work. Or if you wish, repeat the logging and analysis record on, say, a day each week or each fortnight over a whole term (or longer) and see what analysis of that data reveals. The answer is of course that no day is typical. The art of the exercise lies in accurate and honest recording of your actual, instinctive use of time over a period long enough to convince yourself that you have got as near to normality as possible: then don't resist the messages your analysis gives you.

In conclusion on time

So, considering every aspect of 'time' alongside your efforts to delegate responsibility to others is another, crucial, factor in achieving effective delegation. Be prepared for your early steps towards delegation to bring about an increase in the amount of time you have to devote to the particular responsibility you wish to delegate and a probable temporary decrease in your own feeling of overall effectiveness. And (if you can spare the time!) do an analysis of your own use of your management time to see if that throws any extra light on the whole matter of your desire to delegate some of your own current task responsibilities to your colleagues. Even if you haven't time to complete an analysis, be aware of the five categories of basic management activity and use them in your planning towards delegation. It is easiest (and best) to delegate 'administration' or 'representing' for instance; it is more difficult to delegate 'leadership' and really only to be considered when the purpose of the delegation is to further a colleague's development.

Reference

Managing Learning in Organisations, Casey, D, Open University Press, 1993.

Epilogue

And finally, some practical tips

I find it helpful as a manager to have the overall picture of what I am doing (and why) in my mind as I approach any particular aspect of the role. However, having acquired that holistic picture, I also find it useful to try and distil the key elements of that whole in a short series of simple reminders or tips. On their own they are an insufficient version of the full picture. However, as a framework on which to hang your memory when you are caught up in the hurly-burly of being a professional manager, I find they are invaluable.

Ideally you will distil your own list of tips from what has gone before, and my only tip on that particular front is keep any such list as short and as simple as possible. In the meantime, here is a list I have drawn up which you may be able to amend for your own use, or ultimately replace as you become more familiar with the various steps involved in the process of delegating responsibility for some of your work to others. Happy delegating!

TIPS FOR ACHIEVING EFFECTIVE DELEGATION

These are basic, common sense, ground rules of good management practice in delegating – some DOS and DON'TS before, during and after delegation.

BEFORE

Plan

Do think carefully about what you wish to delegate, why and how – including planning any necessary briefing or training sessions.

Advise staff

Don't forget to let everyone involved in the task, or affected by it, know that it is being delegated.

DURING

Define objectives

Do spell out precisely what you want achieved, not just what is to be done.

Explain why

Do make sure your delegates understand why the task is important, and why they are being asked to do it.

Give clear guidance

Do present information clearly, in logical sequence, and *don't* rush it.

Check understanding

Do check that your delegates grasp what they have to do, by getting them to rehearse the task or answer questions. Don't merely

		assume that they have taken in your instructions.
	Build confidence	*Do show* that you believe they are capable of performing the task successfully.
AFTER	Give help when it is needed but	*Don't interfere:* once they begin to gain confidence in handling the task, let them get on with it. They may not do it the same way as you, but this doesn't matter if they achieve the desired outcomes.
	Check results	*Don't disappear:* it's important not to interfere, but it's also important not to dump the task on your delegates. Keep an eye on the results they achieve, and offer further support/praise as appropriate.

'Answers' to case studies in Chapter 8

Case study 1

Approach described = Selling.

New group: new chair: new task: head determined to ensure, etc., but anxious not to deskill experienced colleagues.

Case study 2

Approach described = Delegating.

Head new this time: Deputy very experienced and effective in this task, therefore 'hands-off' approach.

Case study 3

Approach described = Participating.

Quite experienced and knowledgeable colleague – very willing/keen but never before given personal responsibility for this important choice, so head remains in touch with the task and retains final control.

Case study 4

Approach described = Telling.

The coordinator, though probably a very experienced teacher, is new to mentoring. Head is providing very detailed instructions and guidance in the task and ensuring that a close watch will be maintained when the 'task' actually begins. So, for the time being, the head is retaining very firm personal direction over what is done and how.